Drawing Frogs
Volume 1
How to Draw Frogs
For the Beginner

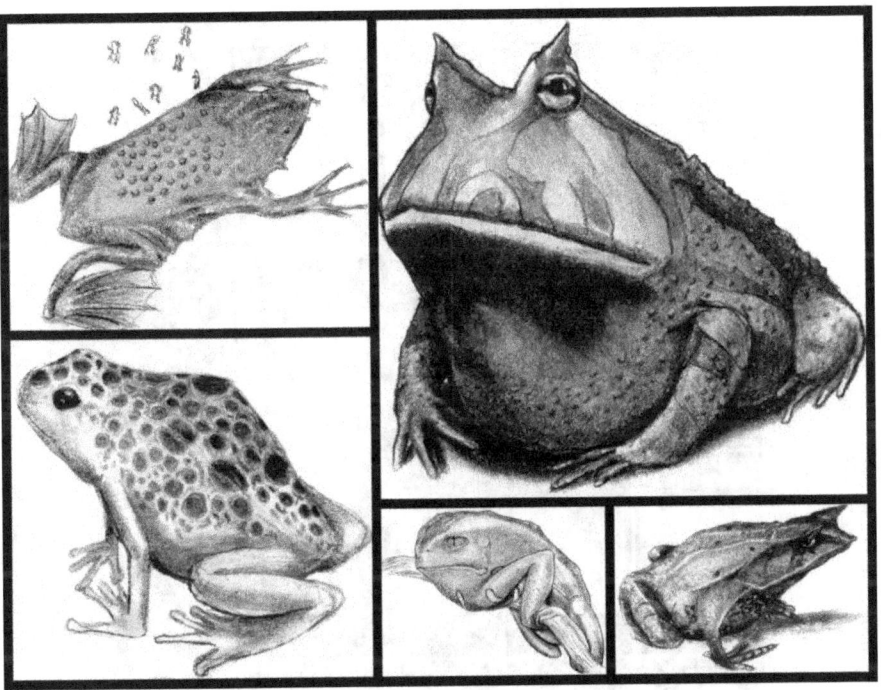

Learn to Draw Series
Adrian Sanqui

Mendon Cottage Books

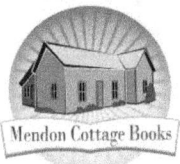

JD-Biz Publishing

All Images Licensed
By: Adrian Sanqui, Paolo Lopez de Leon, Fotolia, and 123rf

Learn How to Draw Books for the Absolute Beginner

Table of Contents

Drawing tools

Pencils

The most important tool you need to be able to enhance your drawing skills is a medium that can be corrected if you made some sloppy line strokes. Knowing and using more than just one type of pencil is a big help and it is better if you have pencils of different grades so you can easily produce the kind of lightness or darkness you want to make. The 'H' engraved near the pencil's tip (side of eraser) stands for "hardness" and it ranges from 2H to 9H. A pencil with only an "H" mark and doesn't have a number means 1H. The most common type (the one available anywhere) of pencil that does not indicate its grade mark is usually a 2H pencil. The "B" marking of pencils stand for "blackness", this means that they can easily produce darker line marks and are softer than H pencils. It ranges from HB (hard and dark) to 9B (very soft and very dark), so when it comes to B pencils, the higher the number is; the softer and darker it becomes. Different brands have different softness, hardness and blackness levels, so if you are going to use a certain brand for the first time, you should try them out first before applying it on your main drawing.

Charcoal pencils

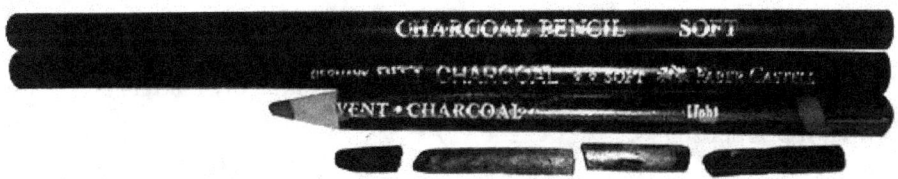

Charcoal pencils also come in different grades. The generic grades of soft, medium and hard are available in different brands. Charcoal pencils are a bit messy to work with; even the 'hard' grade charcoal pencil is still relatively softer compared to those with 4B to 6B grade pencils. It is most advisable for drawings that would require a lot of smeared shading for a smoother and wider portrayal of gradation.

Mechanical pencil

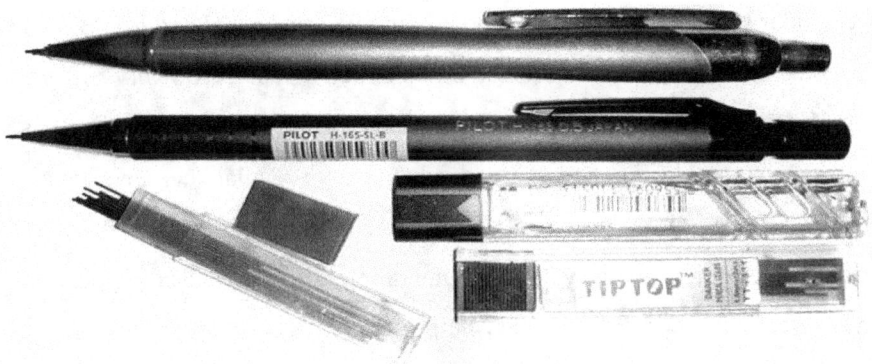

A mechanical pencil has a consistent wick or point which makes it easier for you to maintain the thickness of the line marks you produce. Mechanical pencils are good for small and subtle detailing that requires very thin lines, instead of sharpening your pencil several times just to have a thin and constant fine point that you need. Different grades of lead or graphite is also available for refilling your mechanical pencil, just make sure that the size of the point your pencil has is also the same as the pencil leads you refill it with. They come in several sizes and style, but what really matters is it does what it's supposed to.

Sharpener

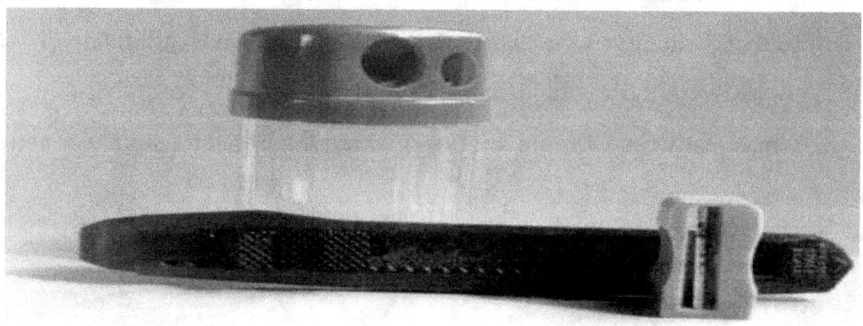

A regular sharpener is quite dependable if you are using H and low B pencils, but if you are going to use it to sharpen a pencil with very soft graphite cores then it may keep on breaking, most especially if you will use it for a charcoal lead pencil. A good substitute for regular sharpeners is a cutter, so you can easily control the pressure that should just be enough to expose the core and achieve a fine point. Cutters are often used if you want a "chisel" point pencil that is very helpful for thick and thin linings.

Erasers

Pencils are no good if you don't have a good quality eraser, having an eraser is essential if you are going to use a pencil for drawing. Choose a rubber eraser that is soft and not the ones that leave a faint color or worst is a scratch on the paper.

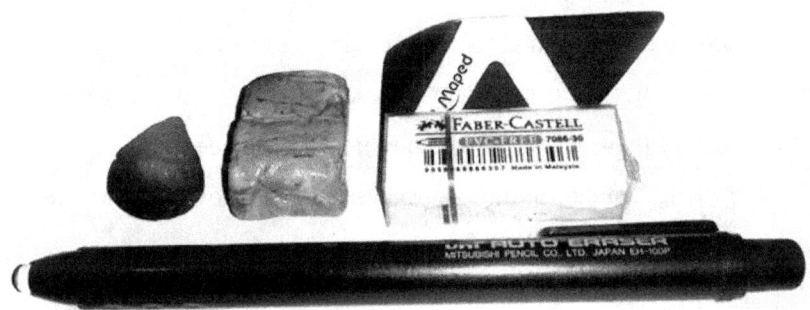

Don't leave your eraser lying around on the table or just anywhere, keep it on a pencil case or anything that can protect it from being exposed on air for too long because some erasers (cheaper ones) harden when it's left lying around because it will dry out and harden.

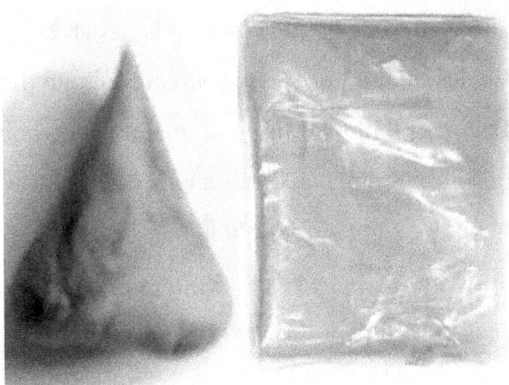

A kneadable eraser is very helpful for making highlights and reaching hardly accessible areas such as the gloss on the eyes or light portions of fingernails and such. It usually looks like a gray slab or a small bar of clay that can be molded or deformed to any shape you desire. It doesn't rub off the marking like usual erasers, but instead, it lifts off the graphite from the paper, like absorbing it. Instead of rubbing the eraser with a certain pressure to remove a marking, carefully dab on the portions you want to erase or to simply decrease the applied graphite or charcoal until you recover the brightness (whiteness of the paper) you want. Kneaded erasers can still be useful as long as they aren't already too dirty or dry. Keep it in a concealed container to lengthen its usefulness, because just like how good it is for absorbing graphite, it would also easily catch dust.

Smudge sticks

A smudge stick is used for smearing the shades on the portions that are hard to access. Some artists dull down the other tip so it can be used for distributing the shades on the big areas. To avoid ruining the smudge stick, use a sand paper to make a blunter tip or to make it even pointier. Smudge sticks or blending stumps comes in different sizes, choose what best fits your needs and it will be a big help for blending gradations. Smudge sticks are cheap and are available on art stores. Common smudge sticks are just rolled and compressed hard papers, so try not to get it wet.

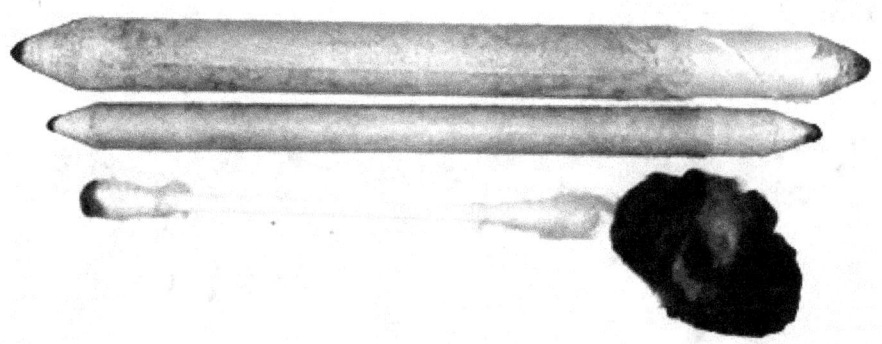

Keep those used up smudge sticks even if it's already in a rugged state (dirty or worn out), you never know when it might get handy. Dirty smudge sticks are useful for producing faint shades, and those with torn up tips can make textures that you might find useful.

If ever you cannot find a smudge stick available (although, I doubt this would be a problem if you have art stores near you, and if not, you can just order online. It is quite cheap) you can just make a tortillion for a temporary smudging tool (some artists actually prefer this one instead of smudge sticks). Use a thick piece of paper (like those on sketch pads, preferably the ones for watercolor drawings. Do not use thin and shiny papers). Fold it on one side and roll it up to create a cone, with the folded side at the tip.

Coloring materials

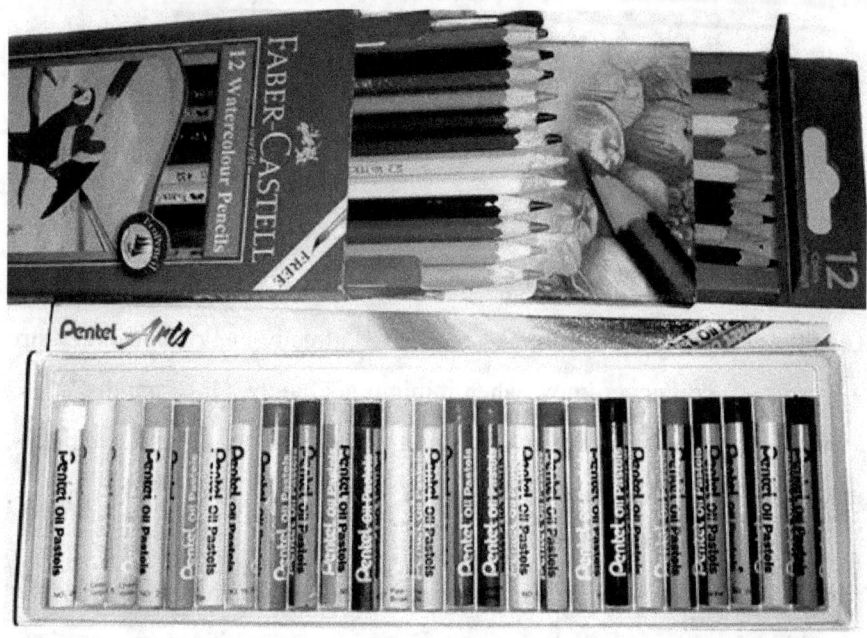

If you are planning to color your drawing, choose a coloring tool that best fits your needs.

Oil pastels are good for blending and synchronizing different colors together. It might get messy on your first trials (if you don't want to get messy, just place a clean piece of paper for your palm rest, to avoid rubbing your palm against the colored portions of your drawing) but you'll get the hang of it as you use it more often. Oil pastels are good for beginners as a practicing tool for smearing different color values.

Color pencils are the next best thing for filling your drawing with colored hatches (linear shading), or even coloring via scribbling. This coloring tool is best for small-sized illustrations. Although, the peak of the tone values that a common color pencil set can produce are far weaker than the oil pastel's, and it cannot be smeared (but there are available color pencils which can produce strong color tones just like oil pastel's or even acrylic's, but they are quite pricy; like the prisma color pencils). This coloring tool is also a good practicing medium for beginners, and my personal favorite for quick colored sketches or even for illustrations with fairly detailed line work.

Establishing the Shape

Just like any other subject for drawing, the easiest way to establish the form or figure of any kind of frog you wish to draw, is by using the simplest shape you can think of that can represent its mass and structure. Think of objects such as fruits, triangles, or any shape that you can easily render with ease (like a pear or a peanut, a right triangle or any simple polygons).

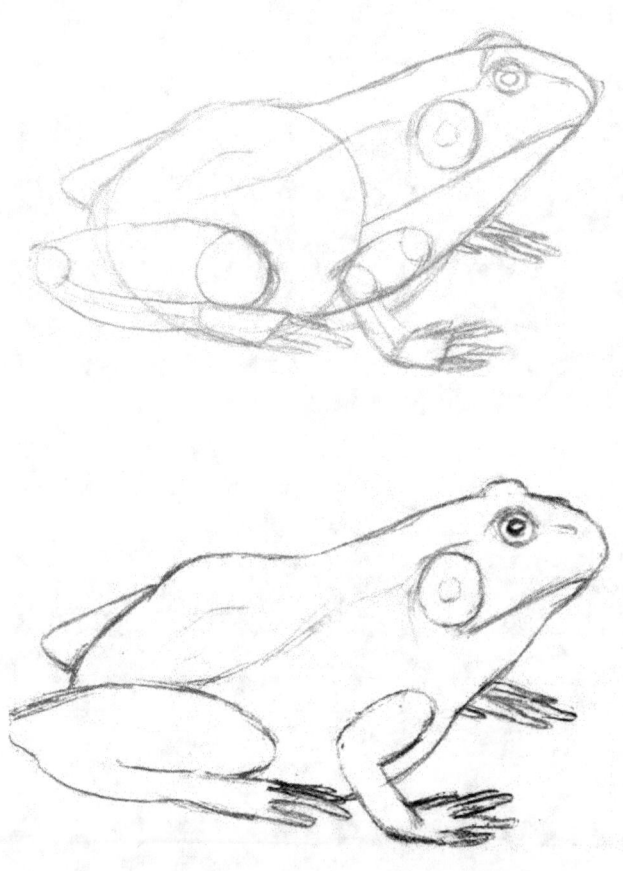

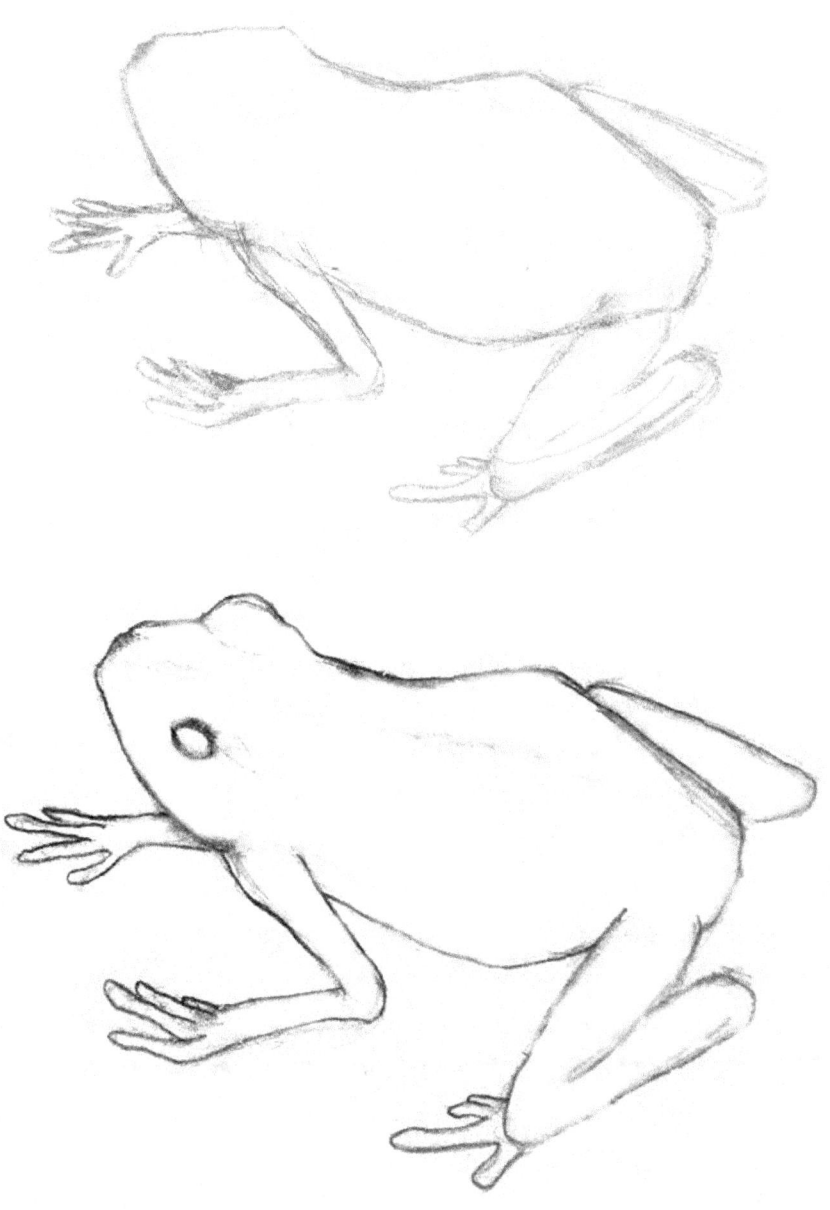

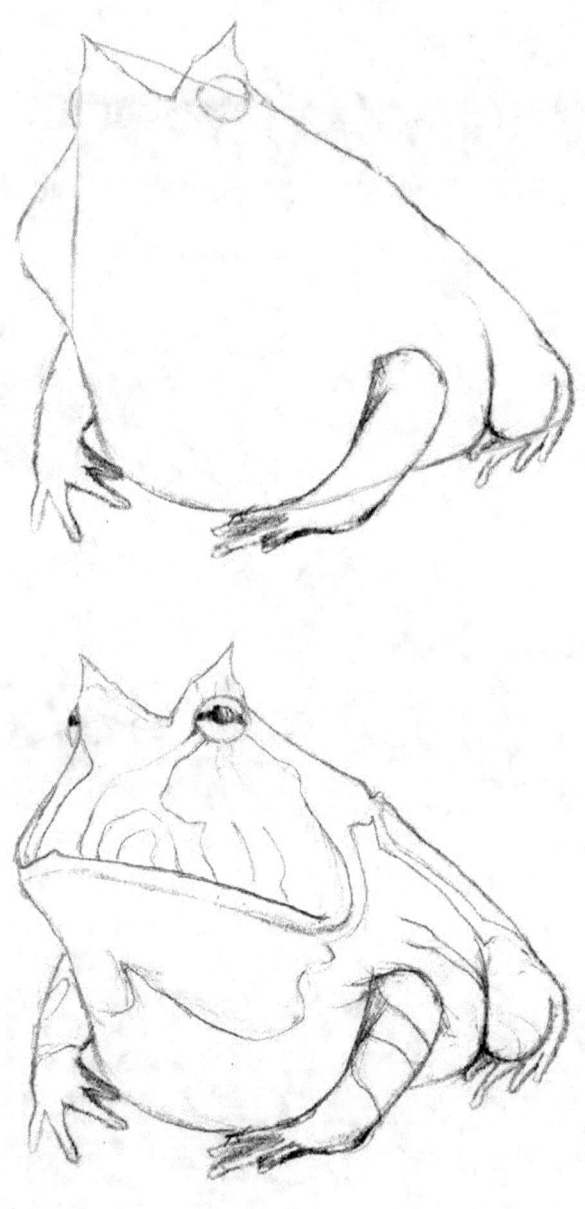

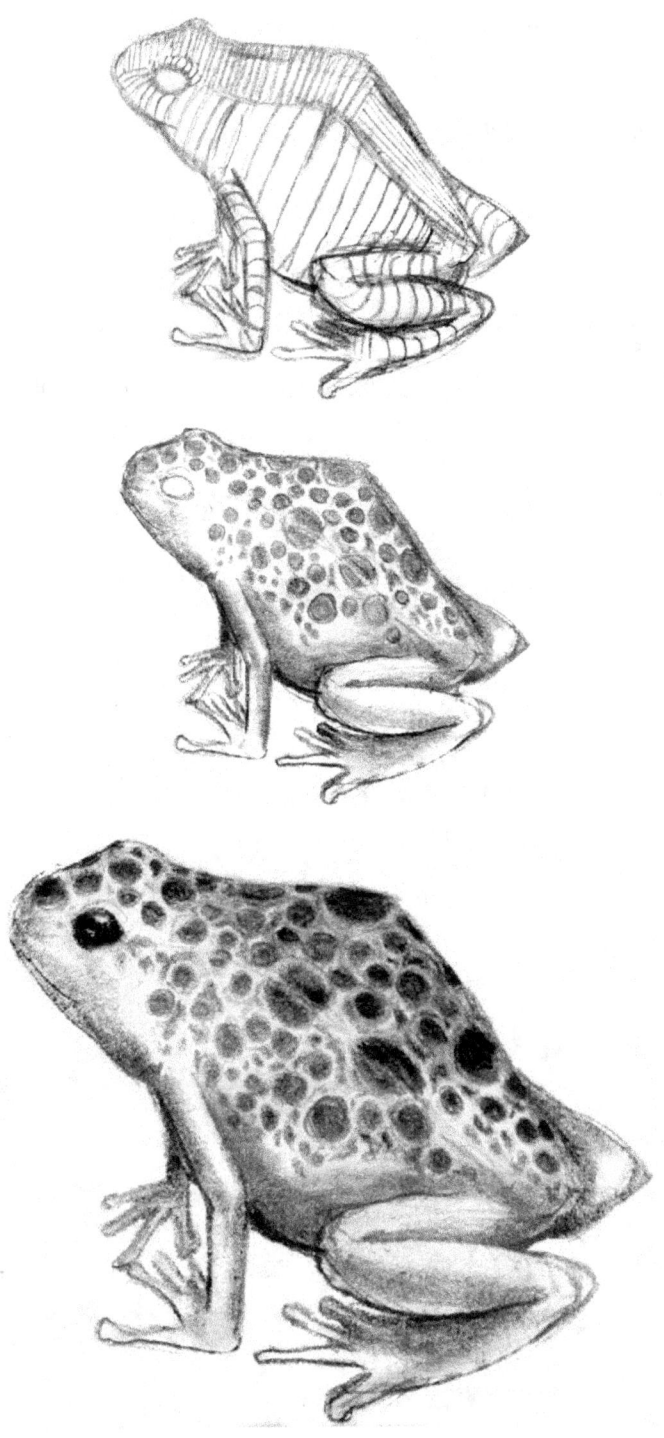

Having a simple and clear understanding about the planes that build up the frog's figure is the key to easily convey the right value of shading and proper way of portraying any details of the body (such as markings or skin protuberances).

- The top plane is usually either the darkest or the brightest.

Depending on the direction of light you prefer, the plain on top is the exposed (in sight) side of the figure that opposes the nearest plane (the side of the figure facing you). And so as the portion of the figure's underside, opposing the top plane.

The sides are often sloped or uneven

- The sides are always curved or uneven.

Observe the contour lines across the side of the first figure, the lines gets closer together as the reach the side edges of the outline, this portrays the portion of the plane gradually sliding inwards.

Monkey Frog

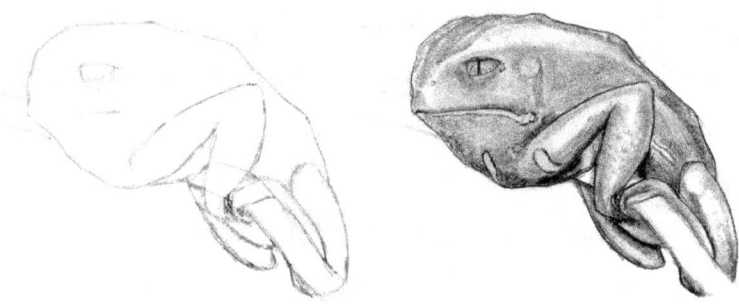

The monkey frog, also called as monkey leaf frog, belongs to the frog family of Hylidae (hyoids) or commonly referred to as 'true tree frogs' (arboreal in nature, which means that they could spend their lifetime on trees). This frog is quite interesting to observe, it is usually spotted in a sitting posture that is quite atypical for frogs. While most frogs are in crouch position with their heads slanted upwards, this frog is actually in a sitting position, with its knees (of hind limbs) placed at the back (a feature that is known to true tree frogs) resting flat, and its head leveled. It has a very calm nature and prefers walking instead of hopping, which is probably why it is often kept as a pet. Some places prohibit keeping this frog because of the substance it is capable of producing. The two type of monkey frogs are common in pet trade (for the places that allow them), the waxy monkey leaf frog (Phyllomedusa Sauvagi) which is also called as the painted-belly leaf frog, and the bicolored monkey frog (Phyllomedusa bicolored). Female monkey frogs can grow a length size of two to three inches, and like few other frog species, males are slightly smaller.

Monkey frogs are basically bright-green colored. The P. sauvagi contains few irregularly shaped stripes of white, mostly on the underside (ventral side) of its body. A white lining is also visible on its mouth that seems to outline the lower lip. Its head is relatively big and is quite unique in shape, there is a prominent (muscle or bone) lining above his eyes which is comparable to large reptile's (you might actually think it's not a frog when you see it on trees showing only its head). Its body (trunk) is fairly wide and bulky, matching its big head.

The bicolored monkey frogs are smaller (in mass), having a slender body shape. The backside (dorsal) is also bright green and the underside (ventral) is light-cream. It does not have line markings on its body dorsally, instead, it has few white irregular dot marks ringed with black, on its underside (mostly below its mouth). Its mouth is not as wide (due to its slender structure) but the eyes are slightly bigger.

- Start with a sketch.

The head of the monkey leaf frog is a bit bulky, the profile is Roundy like a head of a lizard, the snout is relatively less prominent (compared to most types of frogs with elongated profiles) and the brow lines are thick and muscular. The front legs are muscular and fairly thick (for climbing and hanging on trees).

Sketch the figure of the frog to establish its size and position. Check if the proportions are right; if the limbs have their proper length, if the folds look awkward or unrealistic, what portions overlapped the other, and so on.

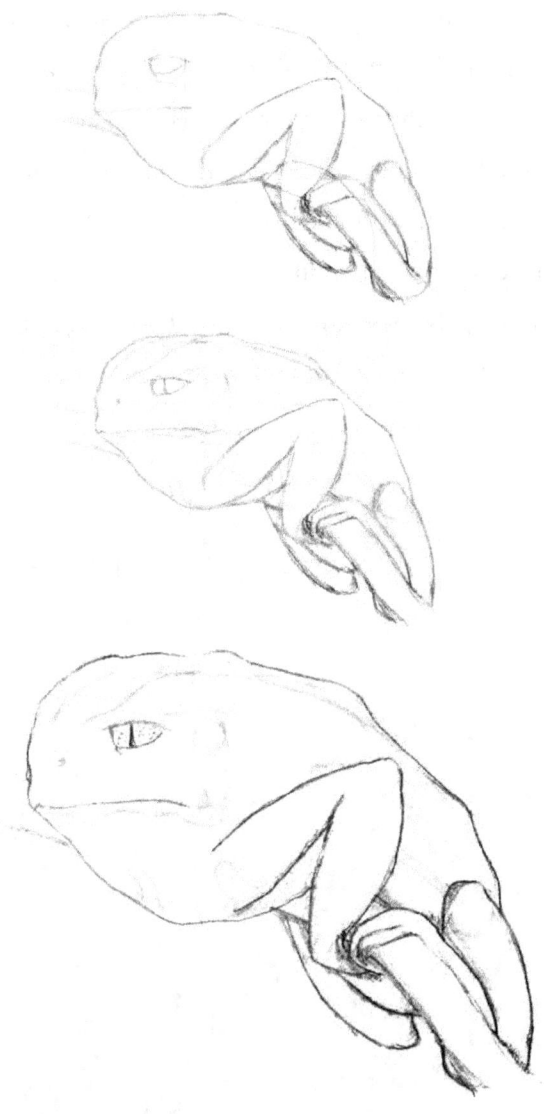

- Redefine the outlines.

Make the main outline of the frog based on your sketch. If you are already satisfied with the figure you drew then replace the best sketch lines you have made with a cleaner and more visible line marks.

- Define the features.

The frog is almost in a profile view, so the farther eye and the farther nostril are totally hidden, draw the facial features on this manner and check if the distances between each features are correct. The space of the lower area of the head should be slightly thicker than the upper area. If you already established the bowline, use it to properly position the eye. The mouth should be at least one eye width apart from the level of the eyes, and the length should slightly exceed the horizontal position of the eyes. The nostril should be just one eye width parallel to the eyes.

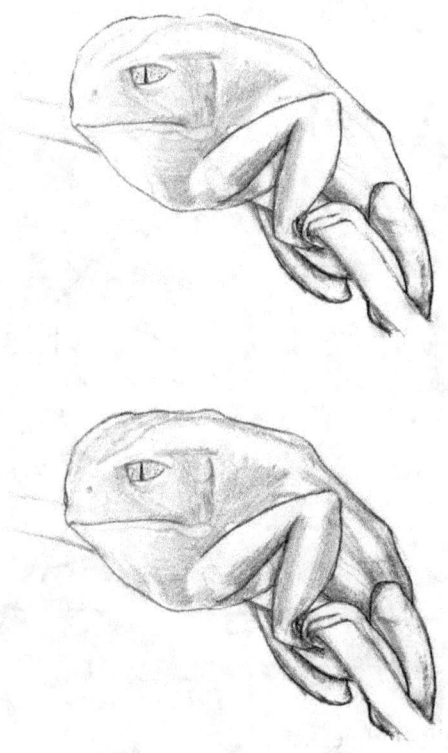

- Apply some shading.

Portray the gradation of the frog. Use the shades to describe the subtle slopes of the body's plane. The directions of the linear shades you apply depends on the area you are shading; even if you are going to smear them later, you are going to need the subtle line shades to portray the faint stretches and ripples of the body. Remember that the tone value of this frog is light (light green in color) so the shading should not be too strong or dark. Aside from being light-toned, it has few irregular white patching on its ventral side, and a lining margin on its lower lip.

You may outline the patch markings at this point so you can avoid putting shades on them, or you can just simply use an eraser later to re-establish them.

Take note of the bright areas you are leaving, these areas will define the subtle ridges on the frog's contour planes (dimensions of the surface). Apply a faint shade on the trunk; curve the row of shades with the contour shape of the figure, the unshaded areas depict the portions with outward slopes.

Apply a row of hatches coming from the edge of the brow line and curving down to the trunk. Also apply a faint shade to the center plane of the head (in between the brow lines), this shading should curve down to the middle of the nostril. There should be a highlight from the nose that connects with the highlight of the brow lines, these subtle highlight should connect to the unshaded portion of the head that extends to the trunk.

Establish the stretch created by the forelimbs by using curved hatches, and then shade the inner edges of the limbs. Establish the joint of the hind limbs with a curved shade line (not a solid outline),

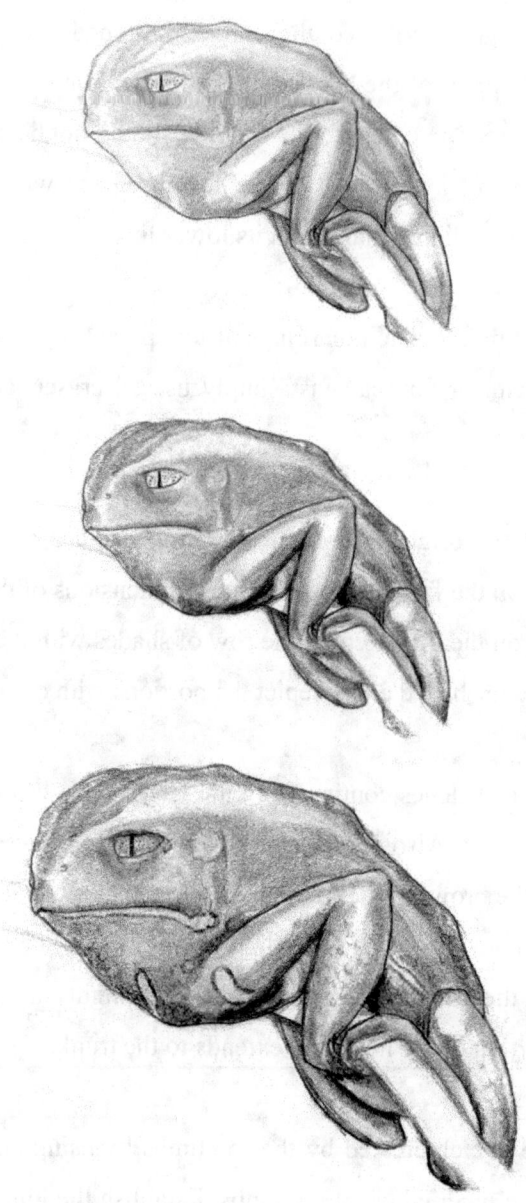

- Smear the linear shading.

Even out the linear shades carefully, take note of the highlight pattern (from the nose, brow line, and down to the trunk) as you diminish the line marks of your linear shading. Remember that you need the subtle linings to describe the stretches, although you can just simply re-establish these minor details later. At this point, the ear (tympanic membrane) of the frog should be visible.

- Darken the shades.

Describe the dimension values of the frog's figure with shades. Amplify the shade values by darkening the areas that should appear darker, and further describe the form of the frog by using different values of gray.

Further establish the marking on the frog's underside by outlining them with thin hatches, and then deepen the lowest plane (underside of the frog). Darken the back area, the plane next to the prominent brow line and down to the frog's bottom.

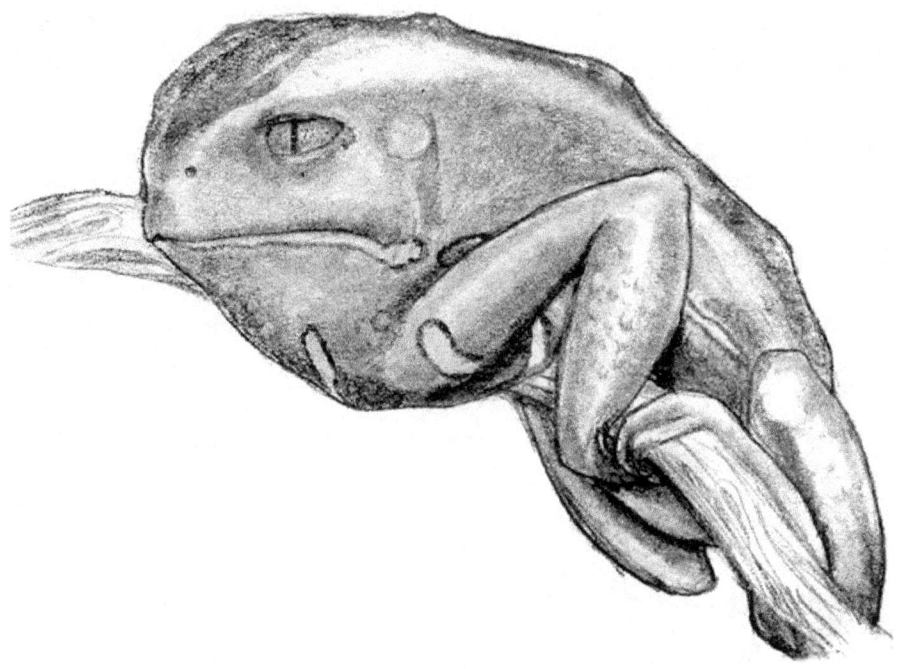

Monkey frogs secretes a bitter toxin that it spreads on its body to reduce the chance of dehydration and to defend themselves from their predators. This contains a toxin that is actually a type of stimulant called dhermorphin, a chronic type of enhancing drug that was illegally used on race horses to improve their performance. It was said that this drug was also used by Amazonians, specifically, the Mayoruna and Matses tribesmen, to amplify their senses which makes it easier for them to hunt.

Pacman Frog

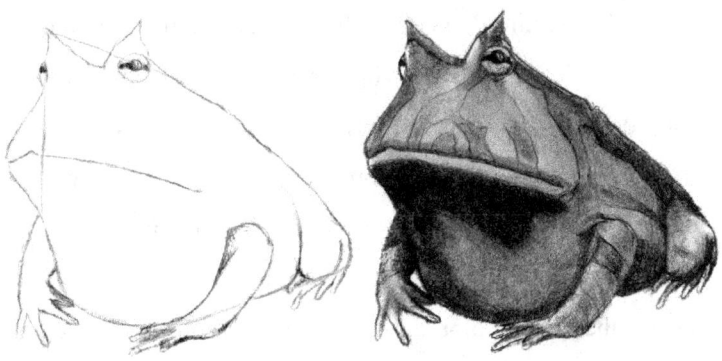

The genus Ceratophrys are one of the largest (in size and mass) of frogs. Some of their kinds (specifically, Cerathrophrys ornata or argentine horned frog, often called as the ornate horned frog) are often kept as pets, because aside of their wide range of diet, they are quite adorable due to their size and appearance. In spite of the name 'horned frogs', not all frogs of the Certophrys genus have horns, or rather, not apparent (horns refer to the spiked upper eyelids).

The shape of a Pacman frog's body is almost spherical, you will barely notice the division of the trunk from the head because of its bulkiness. Its snout barely protrudes from the round body, slanting downwards creating a large gap between the mouth and the eyes. The mouth is significantly wide, and the eyes are relatively big. The limbs are thick, appearing shorter than they actually are due to the thick skin slightly nudging downwards. The thighs are often unseen or barely visible because of the thick trunk overlapping it. The skin is partly glossy, containing skin protuberance (warts, and in few kinds, small spikes), mostly on the dorsal side (backside) of the body.

This frog comes in different skin tones, mostly containing two different colors and few having one color of different tone values. It could be bright green with brown markings ringed with black or a darker value of green, it could be cream-colored with brown markings, and it could be brownish orange with dark brown markings ringed with black. The single-toned Pacman frogs are often yellow-colored with markings of faint orangey-yellow markings, or wood brown- colored with markings of faint darker brown value. Some of them contain few subtle patches of faint reddish-brown (mostly the bright-colored ones), and the ventral side (underside) of the body contains a brighter color value. There is an irregular lining pattern that seems apparent to all Pacman frogs, there are two arced diagonal markings from the farther sides of the eyes then extending downwards to the mouth.

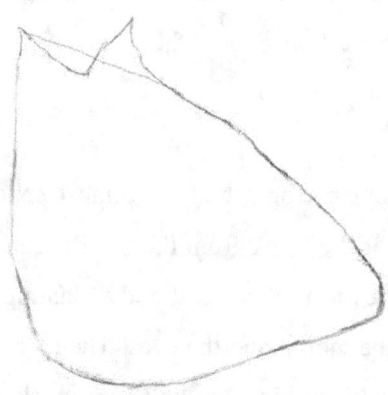

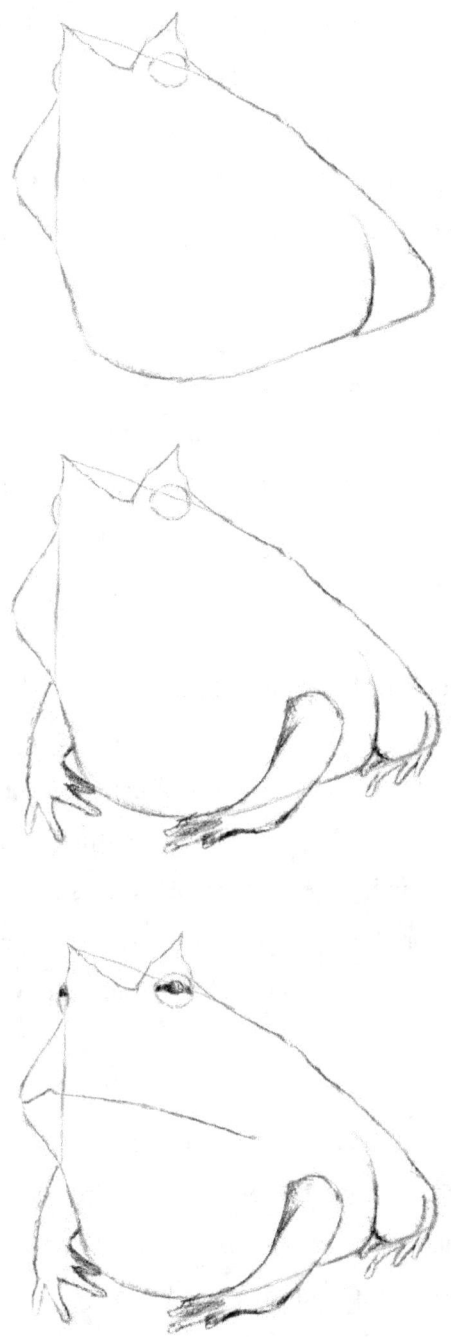

- The bulky body of Pacman frog can be established with a sphere or a right triangle having curved edges.

A right triangle can easily convey the mass of the subject's body, its massive structure is basically spherical, but with a given angle (and this specific type of Pacman frog, the horizontal leveling of the outline from the protruding horns on its eyes and down to its back.

Add the limbs to the base (right triangle or sphere), remember that the legs of this frog appear a little outsized (by the body) and the hind limbs (due to the view angle) should appear smaller compared to the forelimbs.

- Apply the features and refine the outlines.

Once you have established the basic shape of the frog, complete the figure and establish the contour outline of its body structure. Take note of the small ridges and slopes of the outline. There is a small and subtle break from the area of the head and the body (located at the outline of the back area). The outline at the side, depicting the distance of the eyes to the lips and down the belly, should slant from the eyes then slide back below, creating the outline of the lips. The outline of the round belly should slightly overlap the farther leg.

Make a cross reference line across the face to convey the center and place the features properly. Draw the eyes of the frog (the iris has a thick horizontal lining) and the horns (protruding eye brows) of the frog. In this angle, only a part of the further side (of the farther eye) can be seen. The mouth is wide and leveled far from the eyes; arc the mouth outline with the sloping contour dimension of the face, it should be just about below the slanting outline from the level of the eyes, at the small concaving portion of the lips.

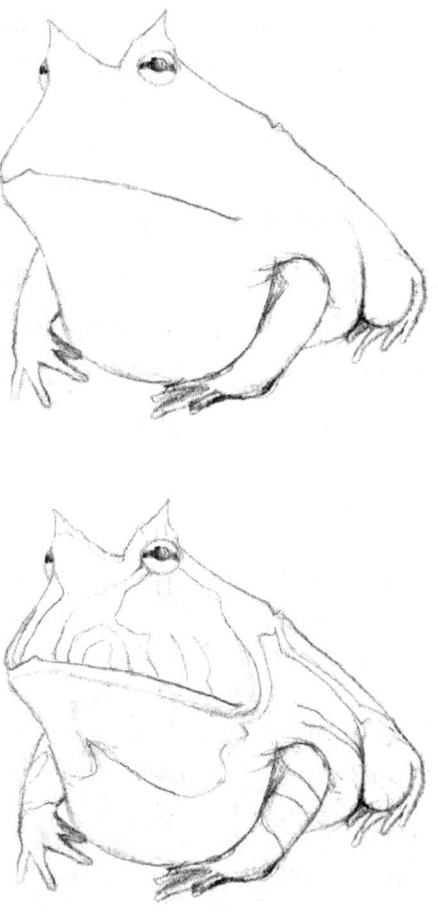

- Add the markings of the body.

The line marking on the body are thick and appears like a margining lining of the features. It is easier to base on a model/picture so you can see how the markings are placed around the body. But it you don't have one, you can just follow this pattern.

There are subtle gaps on some of the body marks, since the color of the marks is not far from the general tone of the body, these portions are faded and hardy observable. There are horizontal stripes of thick lines surrounding the back and down below of trunk to belly, these set of stripe near the margining edge at the back creates a curving outline at the top, separating the area of the trunk from the area of the head. The curved outline is sloped around the entire area of the head, from the horns and down to the mouth.

A form of "V" or "Y" is on the center of the face created by the gap of the two thick line marks, these linings extend from the gap of the upper lip and to the tips of the horns, with an arcing line at the area right above the mouth. These are followed with another stripe extending in a same manner (from mouth to horns), but this stripe is gapped /faded at the center. The limbs contain two to three thick horizontal stripes/patches.

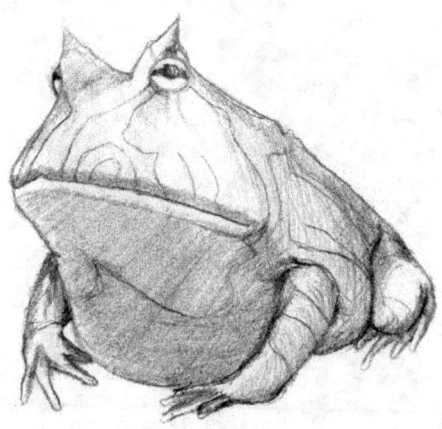

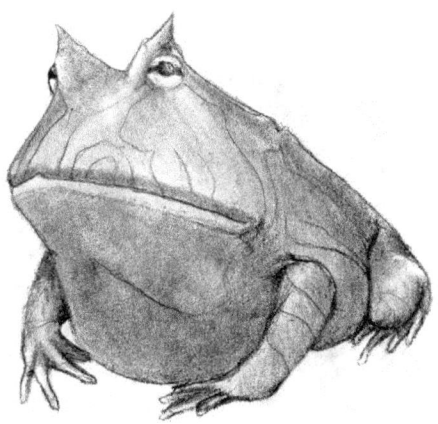

- Start depicting the shades.

Apply a thin layer of linear shading. The shades will depict the position, angles and the surfaces of each plane. Use thin lines and curve them (cross contour) with the slopes, the shifting of each shade values will effectively portray how the planes change in angle. The brightest point should be the area of the head, next is from the back and to the belly, and the darkest plane should be the area from the mouth and below. Shade the upper lip to portray that it slopes inward, the shade value should just be the same as the darkest plane. Darken the inner edge of the trunk's outline, the bottom edge of the belly sliding inward, and the small overlapped areas (corners of the slopes, the farther portion of the end the farther front leg).

- Smear the linear shading.

Even out the shading by smudging each areas separately. Loosen the linear forms of the shades by carefully smearing each plane. Gray out the bright areas with a faint value.

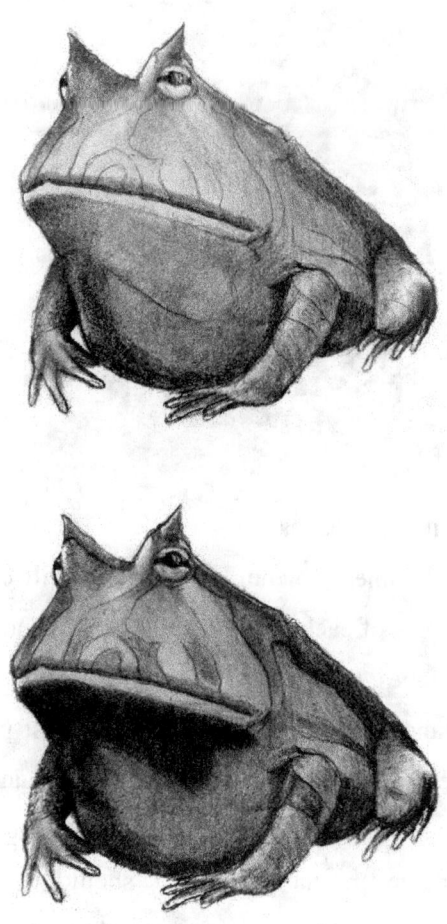

- Darken the tones.

Darken the dark tones to turn the faint ray tones as the brightest value. At this point, you can further describe the farther and nearer side of the figure. Re-darken the inner edge at the back, lowest half of the belly, the plane sliding inwards below the mouth and the farther side down below. Slightly darken the sides of the farther horn, the farther side of the face and the subtle slopes of from the eyes.

- Establish the tone value of the body marking.

Apply a dark gray shading (not too dark) to the markings of the body. The shade of the marks on the face should be lighter as the mark diminishes at the middle area of the face. You can simply use the smudge stick (used) to apply the shades, or apply another linear shades then smear it.

- Add the skin protuberances /warts.

The warty area of the frog is its trunk and none on the face. The warts can be depicted with a bright point (white a white colored pencil, charcoal, or just simply with an eraser) and its shadow (a simple small arc on the lower side of the bright point). The bright dot can be easily done by using a pointed kneaded eraser and then darkening the lowest area for a subtle shadow of each wart.

- Finalize the drawing.

Redefine the blurred outlines and cast a dark shadow to emphasize the massive size of the frog. A heavily darkened shadow adds portrayal to the mass of the subject.

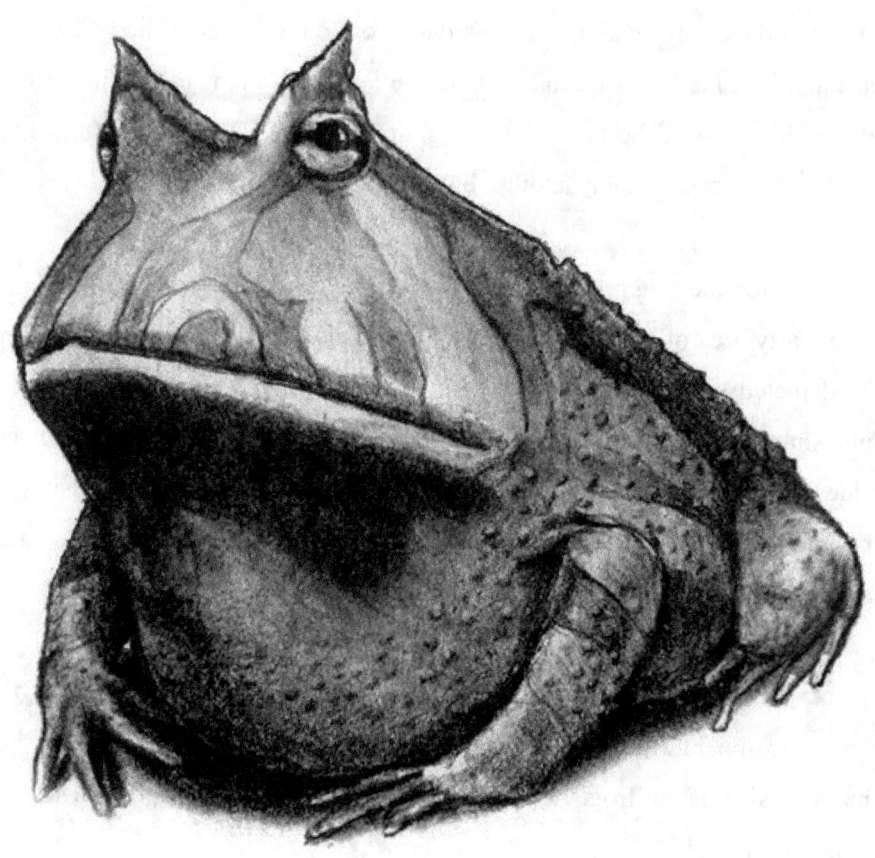

Pacman frogs don't move much, it's probably because of their significantly bulky body. The females can reach the length size of seven inches, while the males are relatively smaller. These frogs deserve its name the 'Pacman frog', because aside from their round shape, they would eat almost any prey that they could fit in their mouth; this gluttonous behavior could also be a cause of their death, as they try to swallow something that is bigger than them, and in some cases, they would actually try to consume their mate (if kept as pet, it is advised to keep the frogs individually or they will try to eat each other).

Surinam Toad

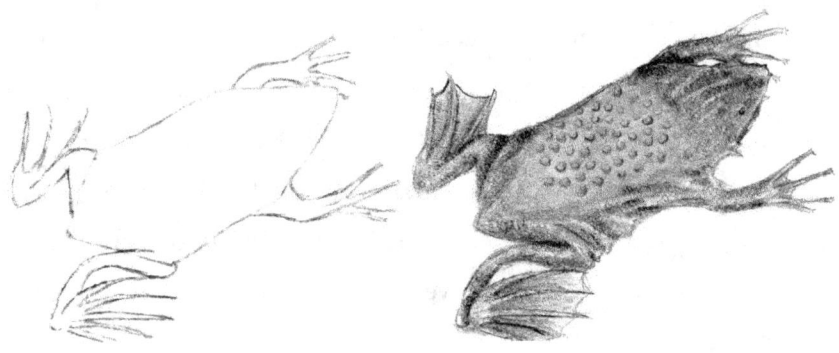

This one is probably the most bizarre-looking kind amongst them all. The Surinam/Suriname toad, also called as the star-fingered toad or Pipa, is a flat leaf-shaped toad that can be found in swamps or freshwater marshes of damp lowland forests in Panama and South America. It is commonly seen on rivers and small ponds on tropical/sub-tropical forest of Ecuador, Peru, Colombia, Venezuela, Bolivia, Trinidad and (as the name says) Suriname. Its body is utterly flat that it's quite pointless to measure the mass, as if a frog got ran over by a truck and survived. The body of a Suriname toad is fixed in a splayed posture, it cannot sit, squat, and it (obviously) cannot jump (it can't even turn its head and could barely stretch its limbs). But in spite of all those incapability, this frog only needs to swim and it is good in doing that, it has a wide (which is also flat) and muscular thigh, combined with long webbed toes. It has no use for any wide movements nor change of body position. It is a semi-aquatic toad, it could last long under water where it usually hides. It has no teeth nor tongue, it uses its fairly long front limb fingers to pull the food towards its mouth.

The flat body of the Suriname toad is basically leaf-shaped with a partly warty surface. The head is fairly small and triangular, its eyes are significantly small and does not contain lids. There are two loosely protruding short skins on both near-edges of the mouth, and a longer one on its chin. The limbs are positioned outwards, with hind limbs being significantly wider and longer (but is incapable of being completely stretched) than the fore limbs. The toes of the hind limbs are webbed and significantly longer. The body color of the Suriname toad is usually dark mud-brown or dark gray, with the ventral (underside) side having a lighter color tone.

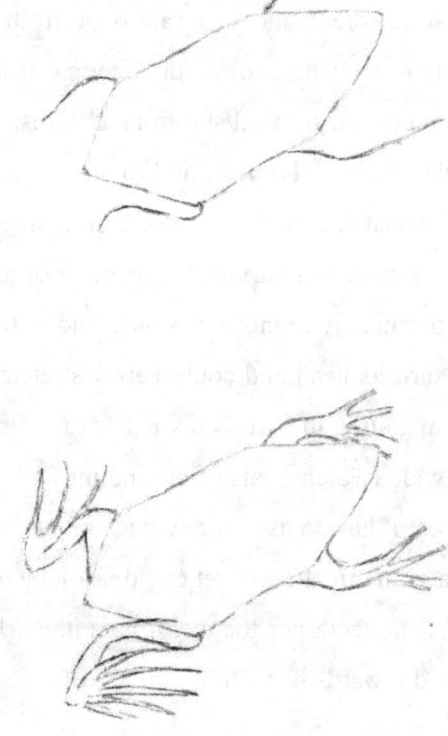

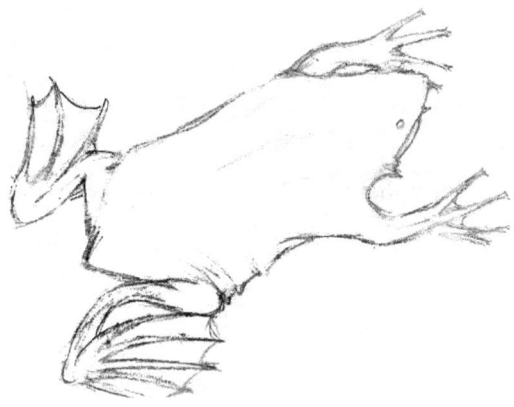

- Start with a sketch.

This flat frog is basically hexagon-shaped, with the head being pointier than the back. Use a hexagon as a base to easily establish the mass of the subject, and then add the widespread legs; in this angle, the distance of the legs from the base is partially foreshortened, the limb that should appear the longest is the nearest foreleg. Take note of the limbs' dimensions; they are also flattened, so the thickness of the sides of the legs are different (like a ribbon or a tape). The toes of the hind limbs should be significantly bigger (wider and longer) compared to the toes of the forelimbs.

- Draw the details.

The outline of the frog's shape contains stretches, ridges and folds. The triangular head contains loose and floppy skins hanging on both sides (at the ends of the head and a smaller pair near the tip/nose). The eyes are dorsally placed, like small pebbles that seems too small for the body.

Add the webbings in-between the fingers. The front toes has shorter webs and tipped with short protuberances/spikes. Draw ripples to the skin at the side of the nearer hind leg to depict its bent gesture (like the toe is about to flap upwards).

Once the main outline is defined, draw the other subtle details on the surface of the frog's back. Draw the pockets on its back (where the froglets come out).

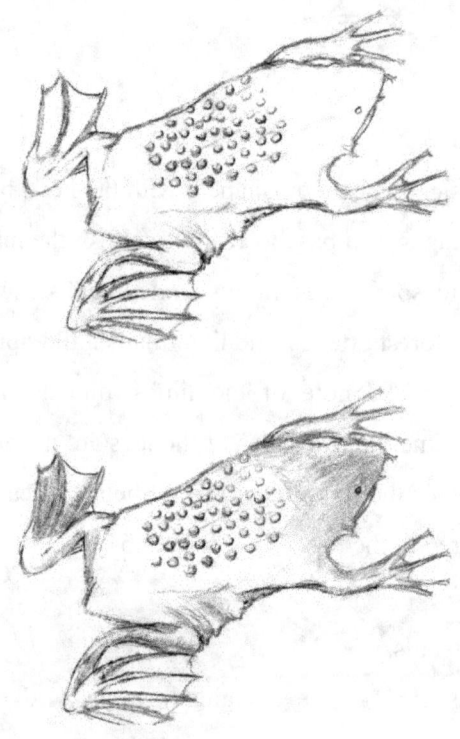

- Apply shades.

The Surinam toad is basically dark colored (although, there are those with brown flesh tones), in this case (pencil drawing), different values of gray must be used.

Start with the first layer of shading by applying thick line strokes with indefinite directions. Use a blunt pencil or the side of the pencil.

Use shading to further establish the ridges of the body; follow the slopes on the outline and convey how the stretches and folds extend farther from the outline. Darken the inner edges of the ripples at the side of the nearer hind leg.

Shade the body while leaving highlights to establish the subtle ridges and slopes of the surface (of the frog). Establish the other stretch lines and shade the inner edges of the limbs; the lower edges and the overlapped areas should be darker. The swollen area (the area with the pockets) has a lighter value, so it is better if this portion is shaded later.

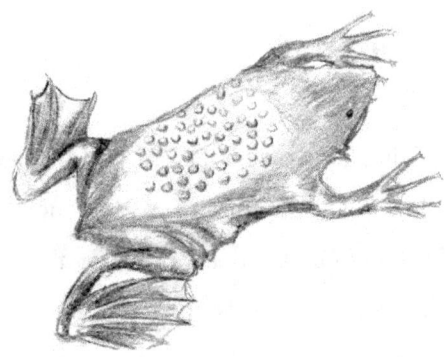

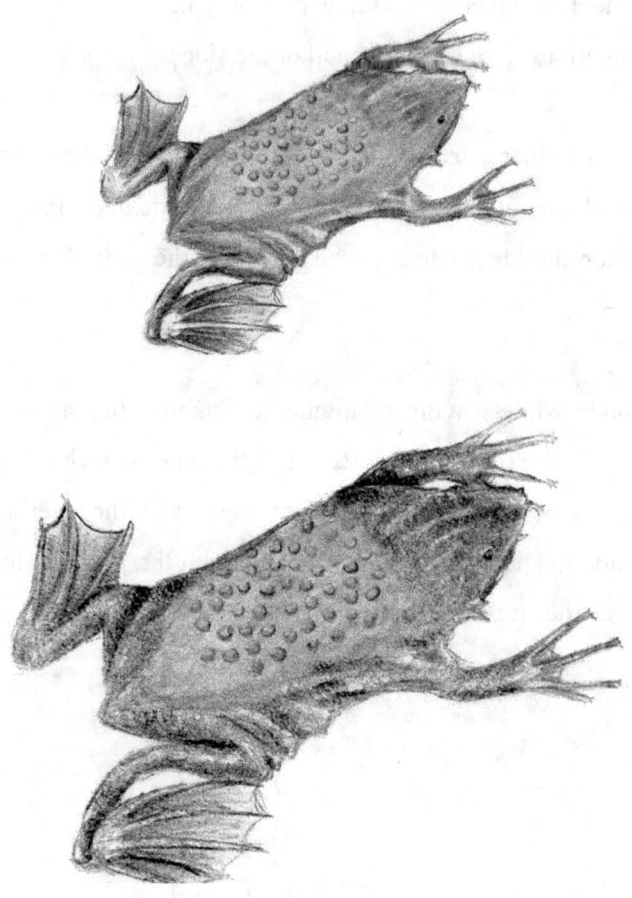

- Smear the shading and apply another layer of shades.

The shading you applied earlier should be the mid tone of the figure, and the distributed shade (by the smudge stick or any of the kind) would be the lightest value, and the darkest value is created by re-applying dark shades. Even out the shades and spread it carefully. Use scribbling hand strokes to properly distribute the tone and produce a lighter gray value for the unshaded areas. Re-darken the darker areas to make the gray tone as the brightest value.

- Define the texture.

Use shading to establish the texture of the body. Apply another layer of shading using small circular hand strokes (scribbling hand strokes). A patterned (repeated strokes with the point of the pencil) line stroke will easily create a warty appeal.

- Finalize the drawing.

Apply some final retouches. Redefine any blurred portion of the main outline. If you are going to re-darken an area, use the same manner of hand strokes you made when you defined the texture. Add some froglets coming out from the pockets and few others swimming away.

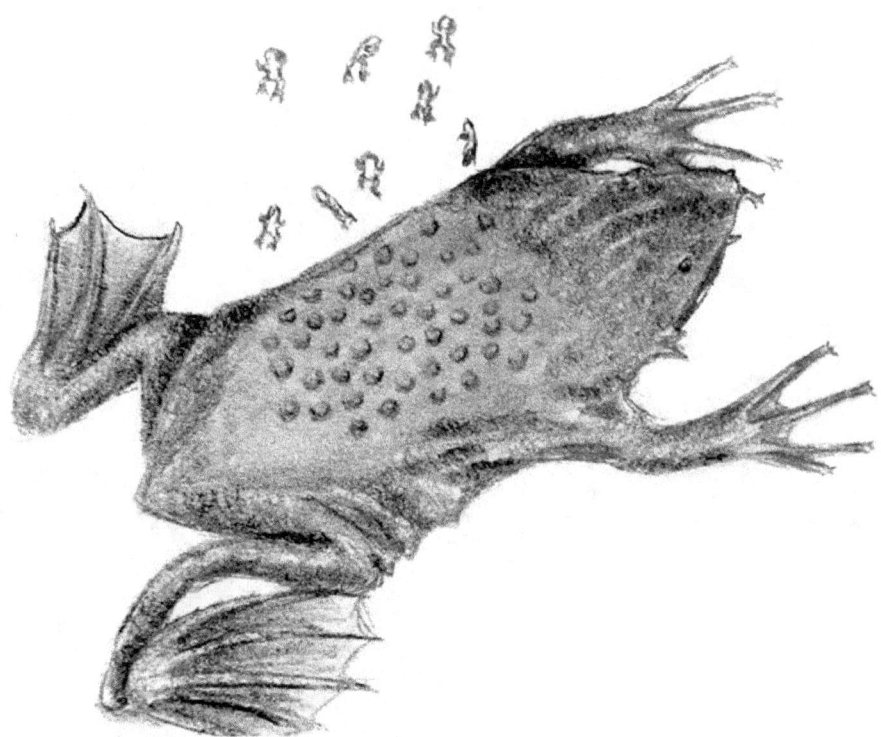

Aside from the Suriname toad's very unusual shape, it is also well-known for its unusual reproduction method. The male Suriname toad will rest on top of the female (and do a number of summersault spins) to place the egg cells released by the female on top of her back. And right after mating, the back of the female Suriname toad will gradually swell, embedding the cells on her back. These cells will remain implanted until they turn into toadlets and finally free themselves from their brooding pouch (holes produced at the back of the female to hold each egg).

Malayan Horned Frog

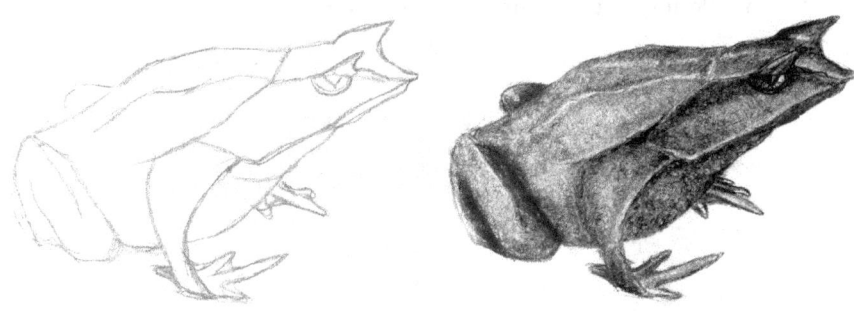

The Malayan horned frog is known for its highly effective disguise, you could barely notice it in the forest as it patiently waits motionless for its prey. The unique form of this frog enables it to easily camouflage itself on the forest floor, appearing as a dried leaf with its wood-brown polygonal body structure.

Its body color is brown of different tone values, from dark wood brown to bright brownish-cream. There are few faint irregular patches of brown of a darker value around the body, making it look like a dried leaf. The form of this frog's body is unique, only this type of frog has this physical appearance. Instead of having curves and slopes to form the dimensional value of its body shape, the composition of its body dimensions are polygonal. The head size is relatively wider than the trunk, having a significantly wide mouth and a pointed snout. The limbs seem flattened and somehow disproportionate for the body's mass. It appears as if it's just an intricate leaf origami of a frog. Its body is wide and relatively big, with an angular contour shape, having different planes to form its structure. The dorsolateral dermal plica (lining on a frog's back) is visually apparent, there are also linings at the sides next to the dorsal linings of the trunk, extending from the lower portion (like definitive outlines of the body structure) and up to its triangular horns (upper eyelids). Its eyes has the same brown value of its body, completing its clever dried-leaf mimicry.

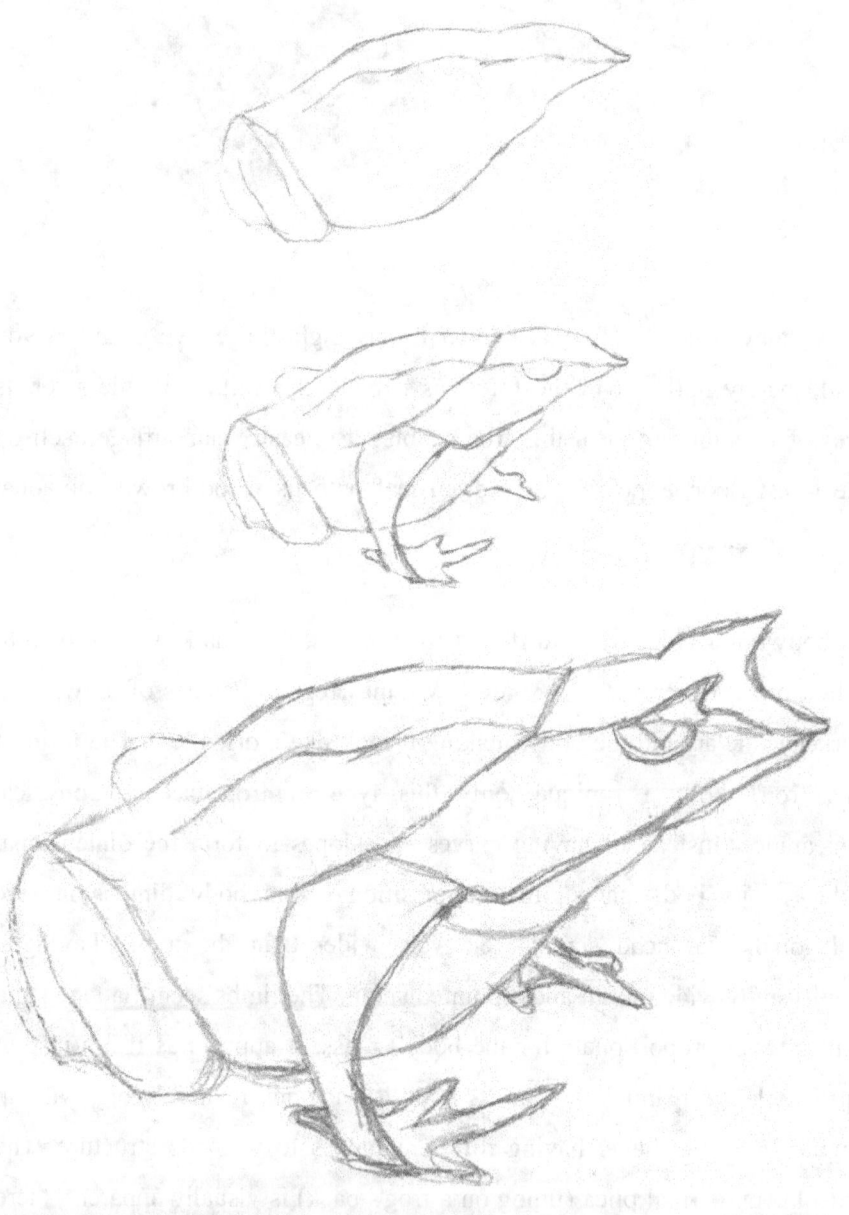

- Make a sketch of the basic from of the frog.

Make an outline sketch of the frog to establish its size and proportions. Just begin with a basic shape for the body and convey the length and folds of the limbs with curved lines. The upper body of Malayan horned frog has a sturdier outline compared to the other frogs; it usually has a curved outline from the back and to the head, but this one has a straight outline. The pupil of the Malayan horned frog is triangular

- Re-define the outlines and convey the linings of the body.

Illustrate the polygonal characteristic of the frog by establishing the planes of the shape's structure. There are three major planes on the frogs figure, all are bordered with protruding skin margins; the back, the head and the belly. The limbs are significantly slim and seemed flattened (imagined a ribbon).

The outline at the back separates the plane of this portion to the others. While side and the ventral portion (belly) can be established with a single curved plane. There is a lining that separates the head from the trunk, and the head alone is structured with different planes. The upper plane or the area of the crown holds the prominent eyebrows or the horns. The sides is also bordered with a lining, the jaw line is prominent and the corner curve is pointed. The under-side of the mouth (throat) connected to the area of the belly also has a visually recognizable outline. These three planes of the head is spear-pointed, creating the triangular shape of the head.

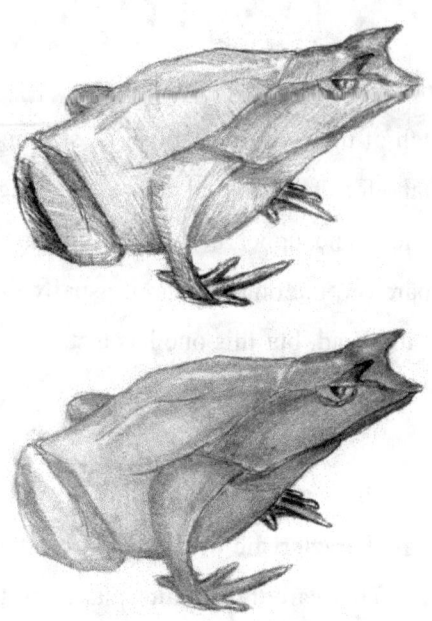

- Apply a linear shading.

Apply some linear shades to create the first layer of shading. The well-established planes of the frog will help for applying its proper gradation, and on this step you will have to convey the form further.

The horn is slightly foreshortened because it is pointed forward. The plane at the side of the head is slightly sloped inwards, so the upper side of it has to be darker. The underside of the head should be dark.

There is a subtle lining at the center of the frog's back, establish this by leaving a highlight as you apply a shade. The closest/nearest plane (aside from the fore legs) which is the side of the figure should have the lightest shade value. Take note of the turned and overlapped areas (of the limbs, and the planes with opposing angles), these areas should be darker.

- Smear the shades.

Carefully smear the shades to blur the edges of the line marks. Even out the shading depending on the area it covers. Use light and small circular/scribbling strokes.

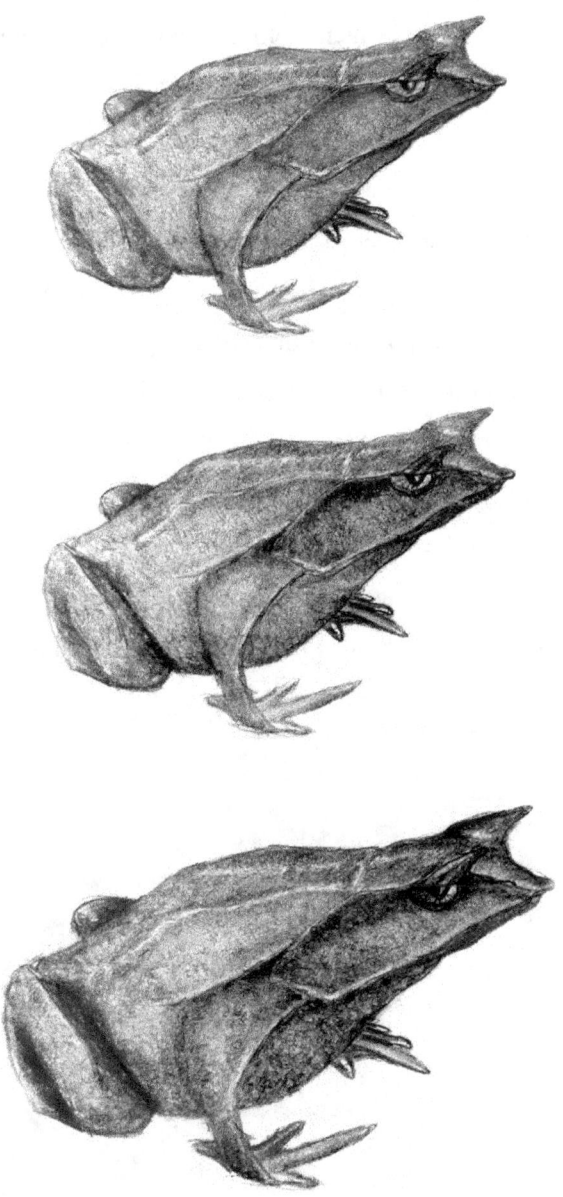

- Apply another layer of shading.

Apply another layer shades to further emphasize the subject's light and dark value. Darken the areas that should appear farther and the planes opposing the light (implying that the source of light is at the front/you). Re-darken the lower near-edges of the protuberant linings and the sloping areas of the planes.

- Use scribbling marks to convey some texture.

Apply scribbles as a third layer of shading, use this as a way to portray the texture of the frog's skin. Use small circular line strokes without a definite pattern; the pressure you put on your pencil depends on the area you are shading, use heavy strokes for the darker areas and use light hand strokes for the brighter or fair gray areas.

- Establish the other details.

The Malayan horned frog has few skin protuberant moles or warts on his body and faintly darker crack print markings; apply these details to finalize the drawing.

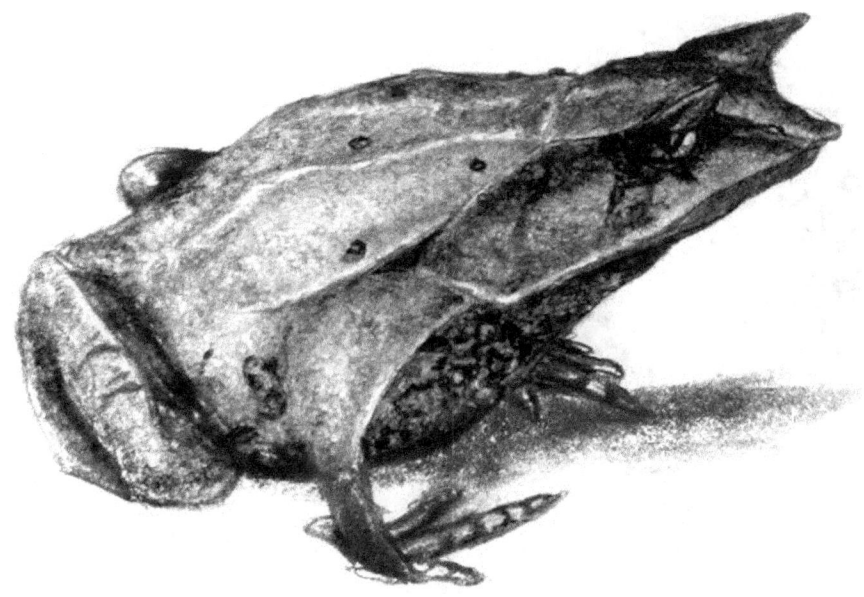

The Megorphys nasuta belongs to the frog genus of Megophryidae (it is not related to the Neobatrachia genus, which are also named as horned frogs), commonly referred to as the Malayan horned frog due to its place of origin and horn-like pointed eyelids, it is commonly seen in Borneo, and lowland forests of Malaysia to Singapore peninsula. Its primary diet is forest ground invertebrates, as well as other smaller frogs and snails. The Malayan horned frog is not an active hunter, it would remain on its chosen spot for several hours and wait for a prey to arrive, then ensnare with its tongue if the target is within its reach. It solely depends on its act of dried leaf-mimicry to survive. An adult female Megorphys nasuta is bigger compared to male, having a size of approximately sixteen centimeters in length, while an adult male could only reach a size length of ten centimeter.

Thank you for reading!

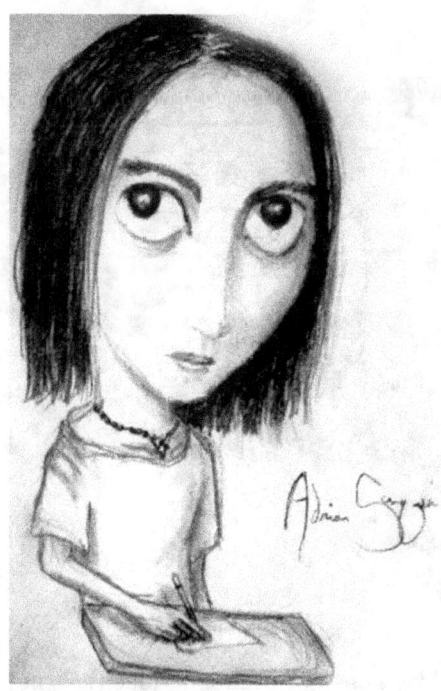

Author Bio

Adrian Sanqui

Check out some of my other books:

Manual Drawing for the Absolute Beginner

Learn to Draw People

Learn to Draw Cartoons

Learn to Draw Super Heroes

Learn to Draw Faces and Portraits

Learn to Draw Caricatures

Learn to Draw Animals in Pencil

How to Draw Lizards

Drawing Cartoon Animals for the Beginner

Drawing Insects for Beginners

Drawing Birds for Beginners

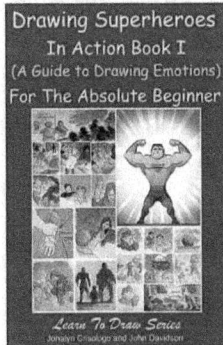

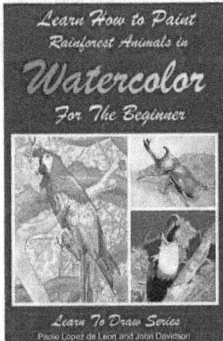

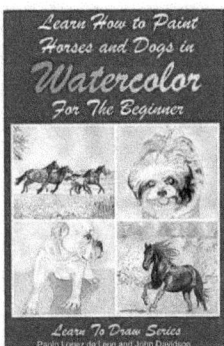

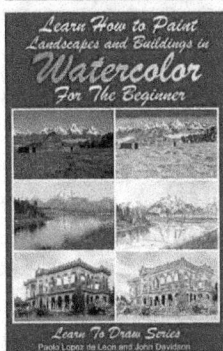

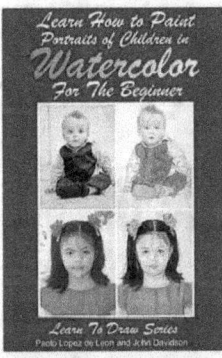

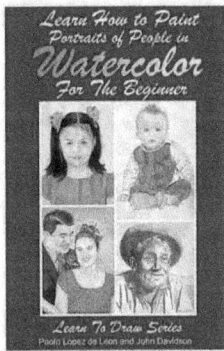

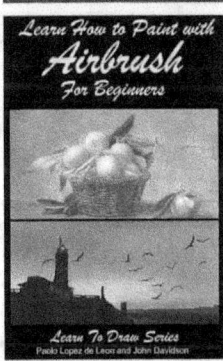

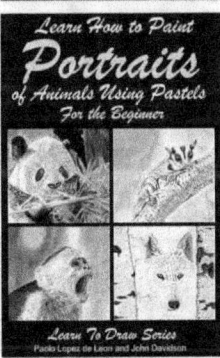

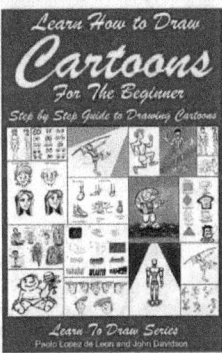

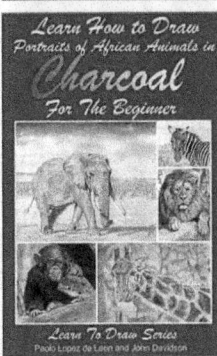

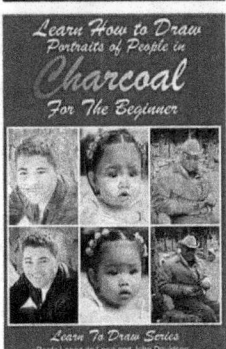

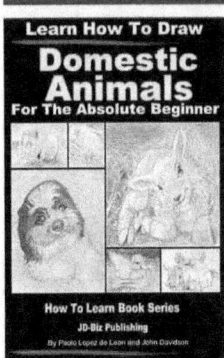

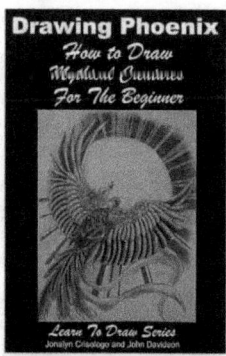

Drawing Phoenix
How to Draw Mythland Creatures For The Beginner
Learn To Draw Series
Jonalyn Crisologo and John Davidson

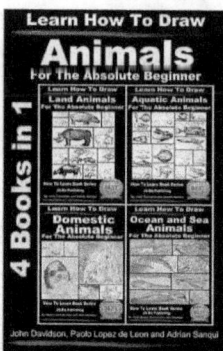

Learn How To Draw Animals For The Absolute Beginner
4 Books in 1
Learn How To Draw Land Animals For The Absolute Beginner
Learn How To Draw Aquatic Animals For The Absolute Beginner
Learn How To Draw Domestic Animals For The Absolute Beginner
Learn How To Draw Ocean and Sea Animals For The Absolute Beginner
John Davidson, Paolo López de Leon and Adrian Sanqui

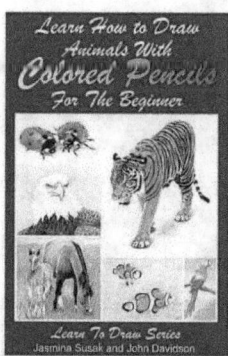

Learn How to Draw Animals With **Colored Pencils** *For The Beginner*
Learn To Draw Series
Jasmina Susak and John Davidson

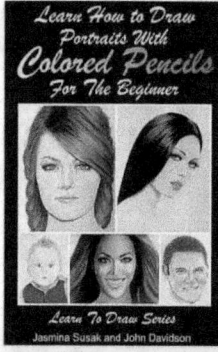

Learn How to Draw Portraits With **Colored Pencils** *For The Beginner*
Learn To Draw Series
Jasmina Susak and John Davidson

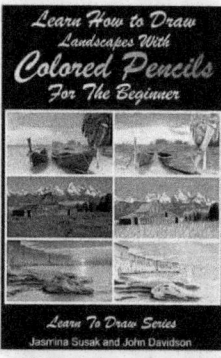

Learn How to Draw Landscapes With **Colored Pencils** *For The Beginner*
Learn To Draw Series
Jasmina Susak and John Davidson

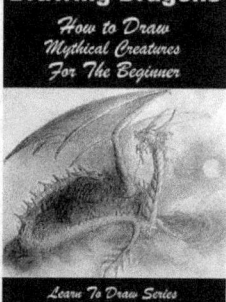

Drawing Dragons
How to Draw Mythical Creatures For The Beginner
Learn To Draw Series
Jonalyn Crisologo and John Davidson

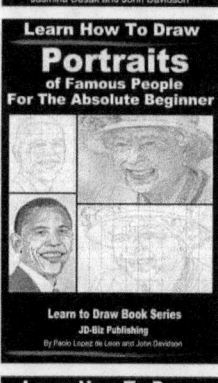

Learn How To Draw Portraits
of Famous People For The Absolute Beginner
Learn to Draw Book Series
JD-Biz Publishing
By Paolo Lopez de Leon and John Davidson

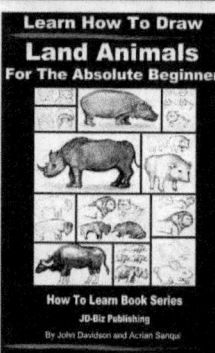

Learn How To Draw Land Animals For The Absolute Beginner
How To Learn Book Series
JD-Biz Publishing
By John Davidson and Acrian Sanqui

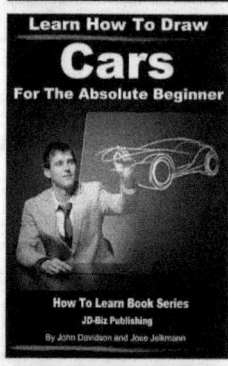

Learn How To Draw Cars For The Absolute Beginner
How To Learn Book Series
JD-Biz Publishing
By John Davidson and Jose Jelkmann

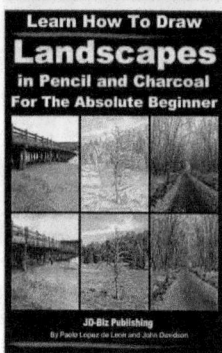

Learn How To Draw Landscapes in Pencil and Charcoal For The Absolute Beginner
JD-Biz Publishing
By Paolo Lopez de Leon and John Davidson

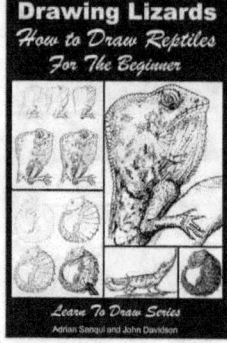

Drawing Lizards
How to Draw Reptiles For The Beginner
Learn To Draw Series
Adrian Sanqui and John Davidson

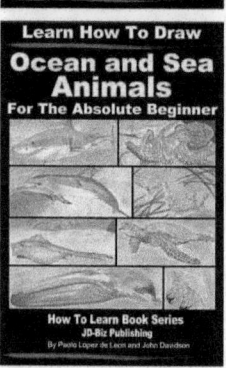

Learn How To Draw Ocean and Sea Animals For The Absolute Beginner
How To Learn Book Series
JD-Biz Publishing
By Paolo Lopez de Leon and John Davidson

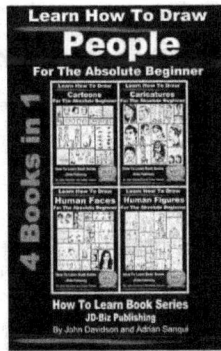

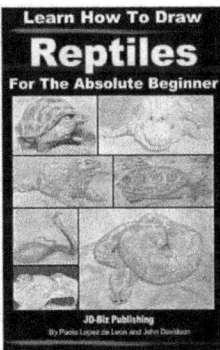

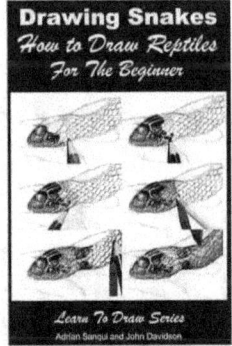

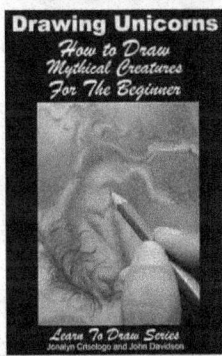

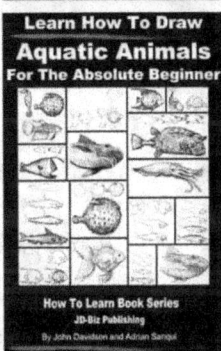

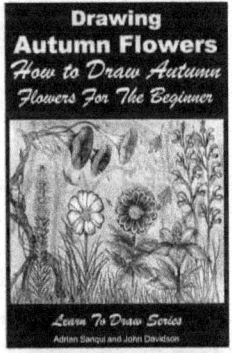

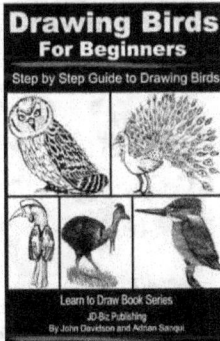

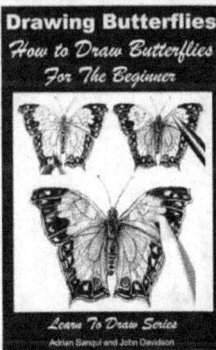

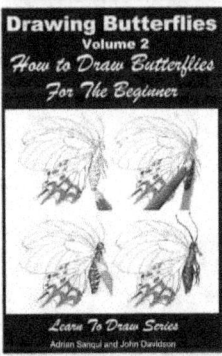

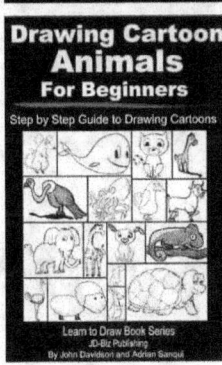

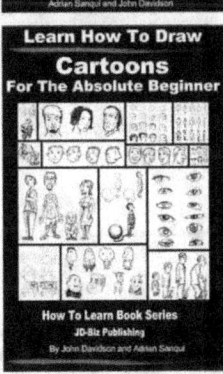

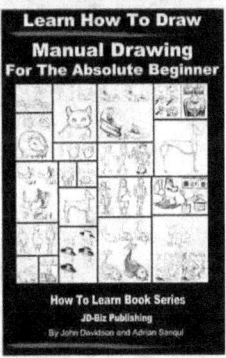

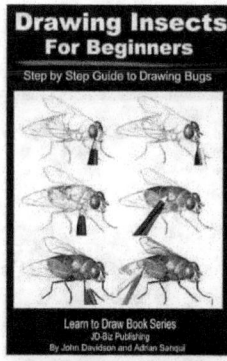

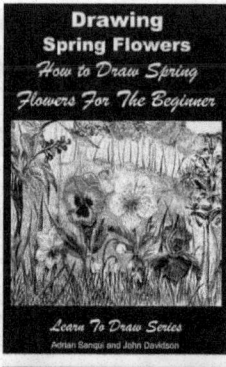

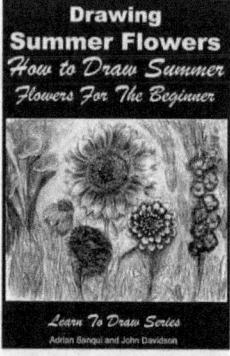

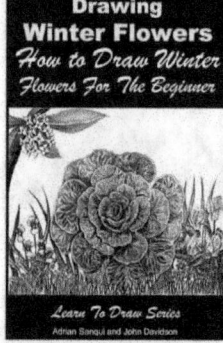

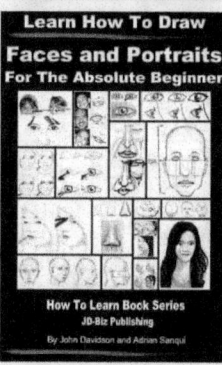

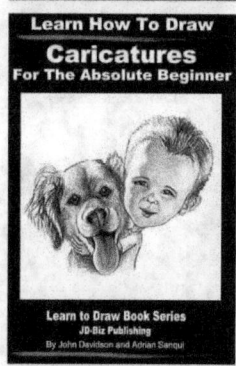

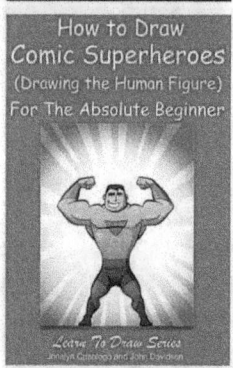

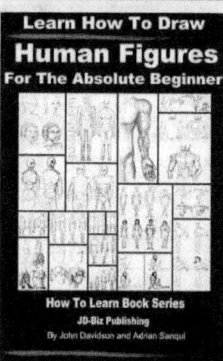

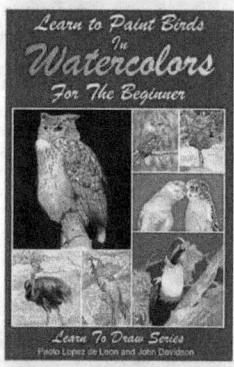

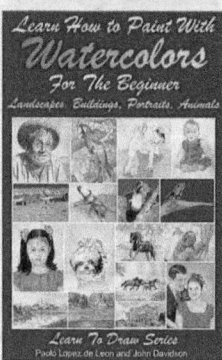

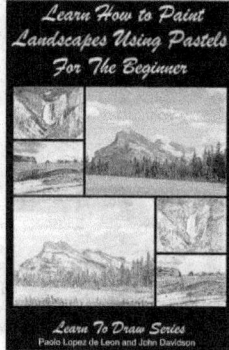

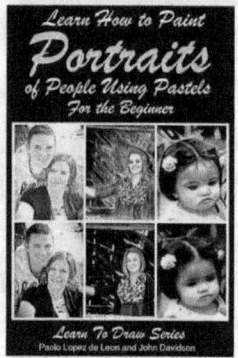

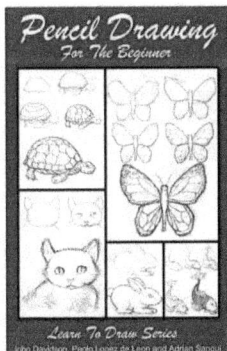
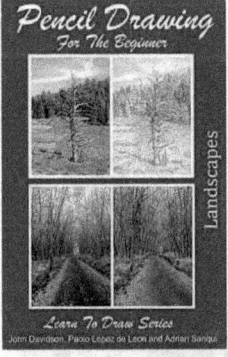
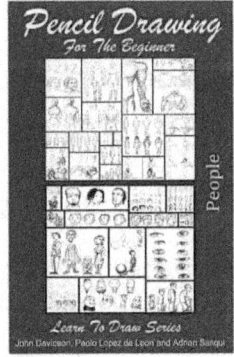

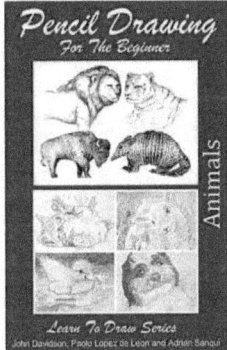
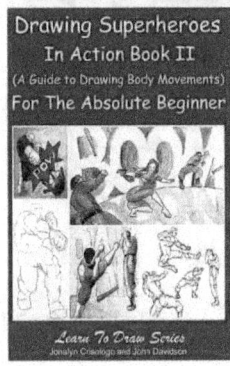

Publisher

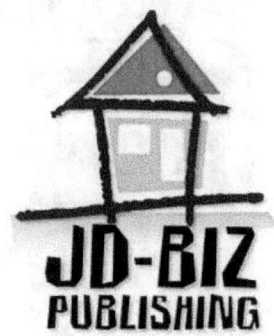

JD-Biz Corp

P O Box 374

Mendon, Utah 84325

http://www.jd-biz.com/

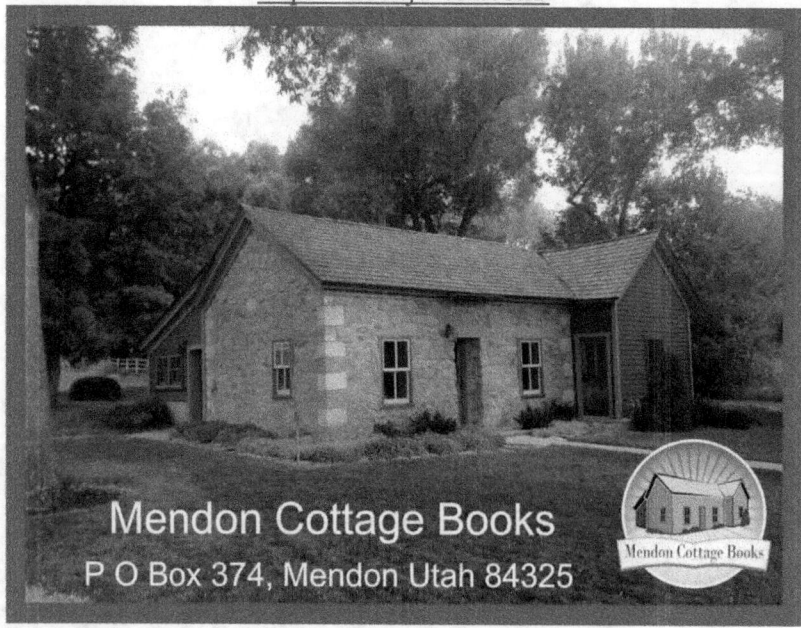

www.ingramcontent.com/pod-product-compliance
Lightning Source LLC
Chambersburg PA
CBHW072310200526
45168CB00014B/1233